This delightful book is the latest in the series of Ladybird books which have been specially planned to help grown-ups with the world about them.

As in the other books in this series, the large clear script, the careful choice of words, the frequent repetition and the thoughtful matching of text with pictures all enable grown-ups to think they have taught themselves to cope. The subject of the book will greatly appeal to grown-ups.

Series 999

THE LADYBIRD
BOOKS FOR GROWN—UPS SERIES

THE BIG
NIGHT OUT

by

J.A. HAZELEY, N.S.F.W. and J.P. MORRIS, O.M.G.

(Authors of 'Drink Yourself Interesting')

Publishers: Ladybird Books Ltd., Loughborough
Printed in England. If wet, Italy.

Every so often, it is nice to have a big night out.

It is important to let your hair down.

And for a friend to hold it out o the way later while you are sick.

Going out to the pub is more expensive than drinking at home.

It is also hard to get a table and too noisy to hear yourself speak and the toilets are worse and it takes a long time to get served and it closes before you have quite finished enjoying yourself and it is hard to get home from and sometimes there is a fight.

The pub is the heart of the community.

Mandy has been looking forward to her big night out all week.

She dances and drinks and laughs and sings. She feels like herself for the first time in days.

Tomorrow, every single thing she remembers doing will embarrass her to the point of physical agony.

Mandy hates the real Mandy.

A big night out is a time to forget your worries. Enjoy being somewhere different. Do not think about problems at home or work.

"No. I'm pretty sure I turned the iron off," thinks Julie.

In Britain, nobody minds if you drink too much. And nobody minds if you do not drink at all.

People only mind if you drink in moderation.

What are you planning? What is your game? What are you after? Who invited you?

Jane and her friends are having a girls' night out.

They have ordered a cocktail, most of which is ice, and whose ingredients are worth no more than a pound.

The cocktail costs £22 because it has a rude name and they can make the posh man say it.

Horace knows he must drink enough to make his work colleagues bearable, but not enough to make them sack him.

Neil tried to impress his friends at the curry house by asking for an extra—hot phall.

"Any news?" asks Neil's friend.

"The doctor says he is still dangerously red," says the receptionist. "But you can visit him as long as you don't touch his skin."

Doctors currently recommend a limit of no more than fourteen drinks a week.

This limit is the same for both men and women.

To help men feel better about this, their drinks are served in slightly bigger glasses.

Leela is starting to regret inviting
her mother to the hen do.

Zardoz and Rowena are having a big date night.

It is important for couples to do this once in a while.

Splashing out on a pair of theatre tickets, a meal at a nice restaurant, a taxi there and back and a baby-sitter is a good way to relax after all their recent money worries.

"Beer then wine and you'll feel fine," says the rhyme.

"Wine then beer" will also make you feel fine.

"Gin then beer then wine then prosecco then a round of flaming sambucas and a banana daiquiri and a can of beetroot cider on the bus" will also make you feel fine.

Of course you feel fine. You are drunk.

Everyone at this office drink has said everything they have to say to each other by half past eight.

Luckily they have drunk enough to start saying roughly the same things again, without really noticing.

When the bell rings for last orders, they will get a bit cross and try to say the same things one last time, very quickly.

Perry has never liked a big night out. "I'm only staying for one," he always says.

Nobody expects him to buy a round. That would not be fair.

Perry's friends recently worked out that he has not paid for a drink since 1993. Tonight they will be presenting him with a bill for slightly under £25,000.

Tyler is not having a good time at the night-club.

All the single women want to talk about their ex-boyfriends and the DJ will not stop playing The Village People.

Tyler wishes he had stayed at the Wetherspoon's.

"And it was Risotto Wednesday,' he says to himself sadly.

Dale wishes everyone from his team hadn't started drinking at lunchtime.

It is good to know your limits on a big night out.

Agree on a signal that a trusted friend can give you when they think that it is time to go home.

Try not to argue with them when they tell you that you have had enough.

Morgan and Leslie are having the time of their lives.

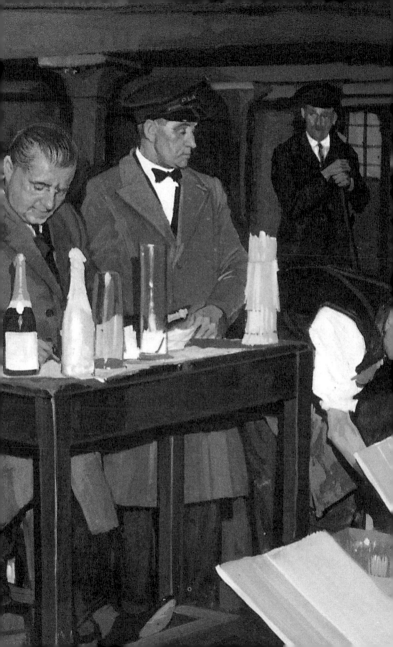

Geef—o, Beansy and The Boy Nutkins are out on the town.

They booked a private booth at a club called Eclipze that promises a personal appearance by one of the stars of The Real Podiatrists Of Welwyn Garden City and two—for—one on Bols.

They had quite a lot of cans on the train and got off at the wrong station. Now they are trying to remember which town they are meant to be out on.

To help your body cope with the effects of a big night out, try to eat a proper meal beforehand.

Green tea is good, and water with lemon, for the liver. Healthy fats are found in salmon and avocado. Turmeric, kale, broccoli and beetroot can also balance the effects of drinking.

A great many crisps tipped out onto the pub table at about half past nine will probably work too.

Moving to a different venue can break up a big night out. The fresh air helps you make clear decisions about what to do next and when to go home.

Tynwald has woken up on the battlements above the postern of Caernarfon Castle.

"I think I can see my shoe" says Tynwald. "In the moat."

He is glad he paced himself.

This HR department is doing a pub crawl around Herefordshire.

Each round of drinks is poured directly into the back–buckets.

This way, Geoff sipping away at his half of Tuborg like an anxious vicar does not hold them up.

Mike knew the lads at the stag would not approve of him sticking to lime and soda.

Gobbsy and Agamemnon have had a big night out.

Now they cannot remember which one of them was supposed to be the designated driver.

Luckily there is a bus shelter nearby.

Gobbsy smashes it with a bin, and they both get a lift home.